AVERY WRIGHT

Mastering Midjourney AI: The Beginner's Handbook

Contents

Thank You

Dear Reader,

I want to take a moment to express my sincere gratitude for your interest in my book, "Mastering Midjourney AI: The Beginner's Handbook." It means a lot to me that you have chosen to read and explore the topics covered in the book.

I wrote this book with the goal of providing a comprehensive guide to beginners who are interested in learning about the Midjourney AI platform and how to use it for image generation. It was my hope to make the learning process easy and enjoyable, and to provide concrete examples to help readers achieve their desired results.

Your decision to purchase and read this book is a testament to the importance of this topic, and I am honored to have the opportunity to share my knowledge and experience with you. I hope that the information provided in the book has been valuable and that it has helped you to master the Midjourney AI platform and achieve your image generation goals.

Thank you again for your interest in my book, and I hope that it has provided you with valuable insights and information.

Best regards,
 Avery Wright

Update for Midjourney AI Version 4

Current Model

The Midjourney V4 model is an entirely new codebase and brand-new AI architecture designed by Midjourney and trained on the new Midjourney AI supercluster. The latest Midjourney model has more knowledge of creatures, places, objects, and more. It's much better at getting small details right and can handle complex prompts with multiple characters or objects. The Version 4 model supports advanced functionality like image prompting and multi-prompts.

This model has very high Coherency and excels with Image Prompts.

We are excited to announce that this book has been updated for Midjourney AI version 4! This latest version of Midjourney AI includes new features and improvements that make it even more powerful and flexible for image and video generation.

Some of the new features in Midjourney AI version 4 include:

New V4 Model

The V4 model is a new neural network architecture that produces higher-quality images and videos with fewer artifacts than previous versions. It also includes improved support for text and image prompts, as well as increased flexibility for parameter adjustment.

Batch Processing

The new batch processing feature allows you to generate multiple images or videos at once, saving you time and streamlining your workflow.

Enhanced User Interface

The updated user interface in Midjourney AI version 4 is more intuitive and user-friendly, making it easier to navigate and customize your image and video generation process.

Improved Performance

Midjourney AI version 4 includes optimizations and improvements to the underlying code, resulting in faster and more efficient image and video generation.

This updated version of the book includes new chapters and sections that cover the new features and improvements in Midjourney AI version 4. We've also updated existing chapters with the latest information and examples to help you get the most out of the new version.

We hope that this updated version of the book will help you unlock the full potential of Midjourney AI version 4 and achieve your creative vision with ease and flexibility. Thank you for choosing "Mastering Midjourney AI: The Beginner's Handbook"!

1

Introduction

What is Midjourney AI

Midjourney AI is a cutting edge artificial intelligence technology that allows users to generate images, videos, and other digital content through natural language commands. This technology utilizes advanced deep learning algorithms to produce unique and creative outputs based on user input.

Purpose of the Book

The purpose of this book is to provide a comprehensive guide to beginners who are new to Midjourney AI or have been using it for a short period of time. The book will cover everything from basic commands and parameters to advanced techniques and tips for optimizing your outputs. Whether you're an artist, graphic designer, or simply someone who loves to experiment with cutting-edge technology, this book will give you the tools and knowledge you need to master Midjourney AI.

Target Audience

This book is intended for individuals who are new to Midjourney AI and want to learn more about this innovative technology. Whether you're a beginner with no prior experience or someone who has used the technology for a short period of time, this book is designed to provide a comprehensive overview of the features and capabilities of Midjourney AI. The content is presented at a basic to intermediate level, making it accessible to anyone with a desire to learn about this exciting field.

2

Cheat Sheet

The Midjourney AI Cheat Sheet

List of frequently used commands

- **/imagine** (e.g. **/imagine a dog**)
- **/help** (info about the bot)
- **/info** (info about your profile)
- **/subscribe** (subscribe to the bot)
- **/fast** (your jobs will be incrementally billed)
- **/relax** (your jobs do not cost, but takes longer to generate)
- **/show** <jobid> (revive any job)
- **/private** (your jobs are private)
- **/public** (your jobs are public)

Explanation of each command

1. **/imagine:** The main command used to generate images based on the prompt you provide. You can also add parameters to this command to specify the image's aspect ratio,

size, randomness, etc.

2. **/help:** Displays information about the bot and how to use it.

3. **/info:** Displays information about your profile, such as your subscription status, the number of jobs you've generated, etc.

4. **/subscribe:** Allows you to subscribe to the bot and receive updates about new features, improvements, etc.

5. **/fast:** This command makes your jobs incrementally billed, meaning that you'll be charged for the time it takes to generate each image, rather than all at once.

6. **/relax:** This command makes your jobs cost free but takes longer to generate the image.

7. **/show <jobid>:** This command revives any job that you've previously generated. You just need to provide the job ID for the image you want to revive.

8. **/private:** This command makes your jobs private, meaning that only you will be able to see them.

9. **/public**: This command makes your jobs public, meaning that anyone can view them.

Examples of each command in use

1. **/imagine:** /imagine a dog - -q4 - -iw 0.25
2. **/help:** /help
3. **/info:** /info
4. **/subscribe:** /subscribe
5. **/fast:** /fast
6. **/relax:** /relax
7. **/show <jobid>:** /show 123456
8. **/private:** /private

9. **/public: /public**

3

Understanding Midjourney AI Parameters

What are parameters

Parameters are inputs that you add at the end of the "**/imagine**" command to customize the image generation process in Midjourney AI. These parameters can help you fine- -tune the image quality, stylization, and other aspects of the image generation.

Types of parameters

There are several types of parameters available in Midjourney AI, including:

- **Quality parameters (- -q):** These parameters control the quality of the generated image, with values ranging from 0.25 to 5. A value of 0.25 results in a faster and less detailed image, while a value of 5 results in a slower and more detailed image. The value you choose will depend on the specific requirements of your project and the tradeoff between speed, detail, and cost.

- **Stylization parameters (- -stylize):** These parameters control the artistic style of the image, with values ranging from 0 to 1000. A value of 45 results in a less stylized image, while a value of 900 results in a highly stylized image. The value you choose will depend on your personal preferences and the style you want to achieve in your image.

- **Image prompt weight parameters (- -iw):** These parameters control the weight given to the image prompt, allowing you to emphasize or de-emphasize certain elements of the image. For example, if you want a dog to be the main focus of your image, you would increase the weight of the "dog" prompt.

- **Width and height parameters (- -w and - -h):** These parameters control the size of the generated image. By specifying a specific width or height, you can ensure that the image will fit within the constraints of your project.

- **Seed parameters (- -seed and - -sameseed):** These parameters control the randomness of the image generation process. By specifying a seed value, you can ensure that the image generated will be the same each time, allowing you to create consistent images. The - -sameseed parameter affects all images generated in the same way, allowing you to create a series of consistent images.

- **Aspect Ratio (- -aspect or - -ar):** The aspect ratio parameter controls the ratio of width to height of the generated image. By specifying a specific aspect ratio, you can ensure that the image will fit within the constraints of your project. For example, if you specify an aspect ratio of 2:1, the image will be twice as wide as it is tall.

- **- -beta:** The - -beta parameter specifies the use of an experimental algorithm for image generation. Using this parameter will result in a different image than if the - - hd parameter was used. The results of using the - -beta parameter can be unpredictable, but may lead to new and innovative images.
- **- -hd:** The - -hd parameter specifies the use of an older algorithm for image generation. This parameter results in higher resolution images, but may take longer to generate.
- **Chaos (- -chaos):** The chaos parameter controls the randomness of the image generation process. By specifying a value for chaos, you can create images with varying levels of randomness. A value of 0 results in a highly structured image, while a value of 1 results in a highly random image.
- **Fast (- -fast):** The fast parameter speeds up the image generation process, resulting in faster image generation times. However, the results may be less consistent and less detailed.
- **Stop (- -stop):** The stop parameter stops the image generation process, resulting in no image being generated.
- **Uplight (- -uplight):** The uplight parameter uses the "light" upscaler, resulting in a brighter and more vivid image.
- **Video (- -video):** The video parameter saves the image generation process as a video, allowing you to see the progression of the image over time.
- **Stylize (- -stylize):** The stylize parameter controls the artistic style of the image, with values ranging from 625 to 60000. A value of 625 results in a less stylized image, while a value of 60000 results in a highly stylized image.
- **No (- -no):** The no parameter allows you to exclude certain

elements from the image generation process. For example, if you specify the "- -no trees" parameter, trees will not be included in the generated image.

- **V1 and V2 (- -v1 and - -v2)**: The v1 and v2 parameters specify the use of an older algorithm for image generation. Using v1 or v2 will result in a different image than if the - -beta parameter was used. The results of using v1 or v2 can be unpredictable, but may lead to new and innovative images.

Version 4 Styles 4a, 4b, and 4c

Midjourney Model Version 4 has three slightly different "flavors" with slight tweaks to the stylistic tuning of the model. Experiment with these versions by adding —**style 4a**, —**style 4b**, or —**style 4c** to the end of a V4 prompt.

—**v 4** —**style 4c** is the current default and does not need to be added to the end of a prompt.

Note on Style 4a and 4b

—**style 4a** and —**style 4b** only support 1:1, 2:3, and 3:2 aspect ratios.

—**style 4c** support aspect ratios up to 1:2 or 2:1.

Niji Model

The **niji** model is a collaboration between Midjourney and Spellbrush tuned to produce anime and illustrative styles. The —**niji** model has vastly more knowledge of anime, anime styles,

9

and anime aesthetics. It's excellent at dynamic and action shots and character-focused compositions in general.

prompt example: **/imagine prompt vibrant California pop-pies —niji**

How to use parameters

To use parameters in Midjourney AI, simply add them to the end of the "**/imagine**" command, separated by spaces. For example, to generate an image of a dog with a width of 500 pixels and a quality of 0.5, you would use the following command: "**/imagine a dog - -w 500 - -q 0.5**".

Explanation of each parameter

In Midjourney AI, parameters are inputs that you add at the end of the "/imagine" command to control the image generation process. There are a variety of parameters available, each of which affects the image generation process in a different way.

1. **- -beta:** This is an experimental algorithm that is used to generate images.
2. **- -hd:** This is an older algorithm for higher resolutions.
3. **- -aspect or - -ar:** This generates images with the specified aspect ratio.
4. **- -w:** This sets the width of the image.
5. **- -h:** This sets the height of the image.
6. **- -seed:** This sets the seed for the image generation process.

7. - -**sameseed:** This affects all images generated in the same way.

8. - -**no:** This allows you to exclude certain elements from the image, such as "plants" or "cars".

9. - -**iw:** This sets the image prompt weight.

10. - -**stylize <number>:** This sets the strength of the image style.

11. - -**q <number>:** This sets the quality of the image.

12. - -**chaos <number>:** This sets the randomness of the image.

13. - -**fast:** This generates images faster but with less consistency and at a lower cost.

14. - -**stop:** This stops the image generation process.

15. - -**video:** This saves a progress video of the image generation process.

16. - -**v <1 or 2>:** This uses an old algorithm to use the last improvement.

17. - -**uplight:** This uses the "light" upscaler.

* * *

Examples of each parameter in use

In this section, we will provide concrete examples of how each parameter can be used in Midjourney AI. By following these examples and experimenting with different parameters and values, you will be able to see the effects of each parameter in action and understand how to apply them in your own work.

Using the - -**beta** Parameter:

Original Command: "**/imagine a dog - -beta**" Result: The image generated will use the experimental beta algorithm, resulting in a unique and unpredictable image.

Using the - -**hd** Parameter:

Original Command: "**/imagine a portrait - -hd**" Result: The image generated will use the older hd algorithm, resulting in a higher resolution image.

Using the - -**aspect** or - -**ar** Parameter:

Original Command: "/**imagine a landscape - -aspect 2:1**"

Result: The image generated will have an aspect ratio of 2:1, resulting in a landscape with a wider view.

Using the - -**w** Parameter:

Original Command: "**/imagine a city skyline** - -**w 1000**"
Result: The image generated will have a width of 1000 pixels, resulting in a wider view of the city skyline.

Using the – –**h** Parameter:

Original Command: "**/imagine a dog – –h 500**" Result: The image generated will have a height of 500 pixels.

Using the – –**seed** Parameter:

Original Command: "**/imagine a cityscape – –seed 123456**"
Result: The image generated will use the seed value "123456", resulting in a specific and repeatable image.

Using the - -**sameseed** Parameter:

Original Command: "**/imagine a cityscape - -sameseed**"
Result: All images generated will be affected in the same way by the seed value, resulting in a consistent look for multiple images.

Using the - -**no** Parameter:

Original Command: "**/imagine a dog playing in a park - -no clouds**" Result: The image generated will show a dog playing in a park, but without any clouds.

Using the - -**iw** Parameter:

Original Command: "**/imagine a dog - -iw 0.25**" Result: The image prompt weight for the "dog" prompt will be set to 0.25, affecting the image generation process.

Using the - -**stylize** Parameter:

Original Command: "**/imagine a dog - -stylize 200**" Result: The image generated will have a stylization strength of 200, resulting in a more stylized and artistic image.

Using the - -**q** Parameter:

Original Command: "**/imagine a cityscape - -q 0.5**" Result: The quality of the image generated will be set to 0.5, resulting in a faster and less detailed image, but at a lower cost.

Using the - -**chaos** Parameter:

Original Command: "**/imagine a sunset - -chaos 0.5**" Result: The image generated will have a chaos value of 0.5, resulting in a more random and chaotic image.

Using the - -**fast** Parameter {Replaced with: - -**quality 0.25**}:

Original Command: "**/imagine a dog - -fast {- -quality 0.25**} Result: The image generated will be faster but with less consistency and at a lower cost

Using the - -**stop** Parameter:

Original Command: "**/imagine a city skyline - -stop 25**"
Result: The image generation process will be stopped, resulting in no image being generated.

Using the - -**video** Parameter:

Original Command: "**/imagine a city skyline - -version 3 - -video**" Result: The image generation process will be saved as a video, allowing you to see the progression of the image. {At the time of writing video can only be made with versions 1,2,3

Using the - -**v** Parameter:

Original Command: "**/imagine a flower - - v 2**" Result: The image generated will use the older algorithm version 2, resulting in a different image than if version 1 was used.

Using the - -**uplight** Parameter:

Original Command: "**/imagine a mountain landscape - - uplight**" Result: The image generated will use the "light" upscaler, resulting in a brighter and more vivid image.

4

Stylizing your Images

Understanding stylize values

Stylize values in Midjourney AI allow you to control the artistic style of your image generations. With a range from less artistic to more artistic, you can adjust the level of style you want in your image.

How to use stylize values

To use stylize values, you add the "- -s" option followed by a number to the end of your "/imagine" command. The number you enter will determine the level of stylization in your image.

Explanation of each stylize value

n version 4 of Midjourney AI, the stylize value has been updated. The default value for stylize is now 100, and it accepts integer values from 0 to 1000 when using the default V4 model. Here is an explanation of the stylize values and their effects on image generation using the V4 model:

1. - -s 0-50: This is the least artistic value, generating images with little to no style. The results are more realistic and less visually appealing.

2. - -s 50-99: This value produces images with a medium level of style, making them less strict but visually pleasing. The results have a good balance between realism and style.

3. - -s 100: This is the default value for stylize and generates images with a good balance between realism and style. The results are appealing to the eye and are not too far from reality.

4. - -s 101-500: This value produces highly stylized images, with the style taking over the realism. The results are more artistic and less realistic.

5. - -s 500-1000: This is the highest stylize value, generating highly stylized images that are more artistic than realistic. The results are visually appealing but may not accurately represent reality.

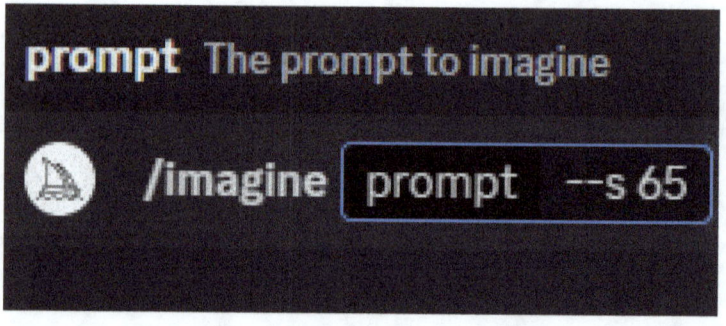

* * *

Examples of each stylize value in use

1. **/imagine a dog - -s 25:** This command generates a less artistic image of a dog.

2. **/imagine a sunset - -s 85:** This command generates a medium level stylized image of a sunset.

3. **/imagine a building - -s 100:** This command generates a balanced image of a building, with a good balance between realism and style.

4. **/imagine a bird - -s 400:** This command generates a highly stylized image of a bird.

5. **/imagine a flower - -s 1000:** This command generates a highly stylized image of a flower, with the style taking over the realism.

5

Adjusting Image Quality

Understanding Quality Commands

Quality commands in Midjourney AI are used to control the generation time and quality of your images. These commands allow you to balance the speed, cost, and detail of your image generations according to your specific needs.

How to Use Quality Commands

Quality commands are added to the end of the "**/imagine**" command. For example, to set the quality of the image to 2x slower and more detailed (but also more expensive), you would use the command "**/imagine <image prompt> - -q2**".

Explanation of Each Quality Command

The following is a list of the quality commands available in Midjourney AI, along with their effects:
- **-q 0.25**: 4x faster, rough results, cheaper
- **-q 0.5**: 2x faster, less detailed, cheaper
- **-q 1**: default value, standard speed and quality
- **-q 2**: 2x slower, more detailed, expensive
- **-q 5**: experimental, generates highly detailed images but may take a longer time and cost more

Examples of Each Quality Command in Use

Example 1: To generate an image of a dog quickly and at a low cost, you could use the command "**/imagine dog - -q 0.25**". The image generated would be 4x faster than the default, but also rougher and less detailed.

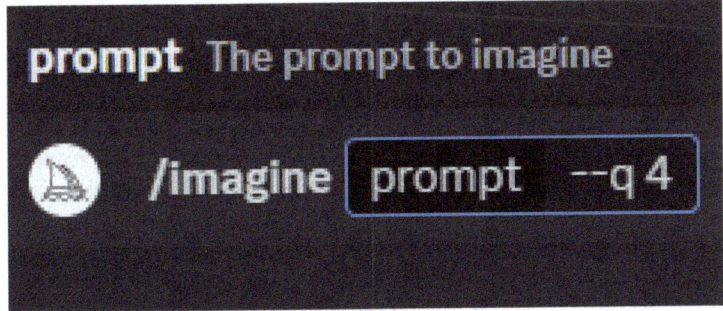

Example 2: To generate an image of a black hole with higher detail and more care taken to ensure quality, you could use the command "**/imagine black hole - -q 2**". The image generated would be slower and more expensive, but also more detailed and high- -quality.

6

Using URLs for Image Inspiration

Understanding using URLs in Midjourney AI

Using URLs in Midjourney AI refers to the ability to add a URL to the end of the "**/imagine**" command to use as reference or inspiration for the image generation process. The URL can provide additional information and context to help the AI generate a more accurate image.

How to use URLs in Midjourney AI

To use URLs in Midjourney AI, you simply need to add the URL to the end of the "**/imagine**" command, followed by the image prompt. It is important to ensure that the URL is formatted correctly and that the image prompt is clear and concise for optimal results.

Explanation of using URLs in Midjourney AI

There are several benefits to using URLs in Midjourney AI, including the ability to provide additional context and reference material for the AI, leading to more accurate and detailed image generations. However, there are also factors that can impact the results of using URLs, such as the quality and relevance of the reference material.

Examples of using URLs in Midjourney AI

1. "**/imagine** https://upload.wikimedia.org/wikipedia/comm
ons/thumb/6/62/Starsinthesky.jpg/1024px-Starsinthesky.j
pg **black hole**"

2. "**/imagine** https://www.google.com/search?q=landscape **landscape**"

3. "**/imagine** [https://www.google.com/search?q=abstract art](https://www.google.com/search?q=abstract%20art) **abstract art**"

7

Multi Prompts in Midjourney AI

Multi-Prompts

Midjourney AI allows you to consider two or more separate concepts individually by using :: as a separator. This feature, known as Multi Prompts, allows you to assign relative importance to different parts of a prompt and generate more specific images.

Multi-Prompt Basics

To separate a prompt into different parts, you can add a double colon :: to the prompt. For example, the prompt "**hot dog**" is considered as a single concept and will generate images of tasty hotdogs. However, if the prompt is separated into two parts, "**hot:: dog**" both concepts will be considered separately, producing an image of a dog that is warm.

Multi prompts are compatible with Model Versions 1, 2, 3, 4 and Niji. Any parameters are still added to the end of the prompt.

Prompt Weights

When using the double colon :: to separate a prompt, you can add a number immediately after the double colon to assign a relative importance to that part of the prompt. For example, the prompt "**hot:: dog**" will generate a dog that is hot. However, changing the prompt to "**hot::2 dog**" will make the word "**hot**" twice as important as the word "**dog**," producing an image of a dog that is very hot.

Note: Model Versions 1, 2, and 3 only accept whole numbers as weights. Model Version 4 can accept decimal places for weights. Non-specified weights default to 1.

Negative Prompt Weights

Negative weights can also be added to prompts to remove unwanted elements. The sum of all weights must be a positive number. For example, the prompt "**vibrant tulip fields**" will generate a range of colored tulips. However, the prompt "**vibrant tulip fields:: red::-.5**" will produce tulip fields with less likelihood of the color red.

The - -**no** Parameter The - -**no** parameter is the same as weighing a part of a multi prompt to "-.5". For example, "**vibrant tulip fields:: red::-.5**" is the same as "**vibrant tulip fields - -no red.**"

Examples of Multi Prompts in Use

Example 1: To generate an image of a hot dog that you eat, use the following command: "**/imagine hot dog**"

"hot dog"

Example 2: To generate an image of a dog that is warm, use the following command: "**/imagine hot:: dog**"

"hot::dog"

Example 3: To generate an image of a dog that is very hot, use the following command: "**/imagine hot::2 dog**"

"hot::2 dog"

8

Midjourney AI Preferences and Settings

Understanding Preferences and Settings

In Midjourney AI, preferences and settings allow you to customize the way the software behaves. With these options, you can adjust the way images are generated, stylized, and exported.

How to Access and Use Preferences and Settings

To access and use the preferences and settings in Midjourney AI, follow these steps:
1. Open the Midjourney AI software
2. Click on the "Preferences" or "Settings" button
3. You will be presented with a list of options to choose from
4. Adjust the preferences and settings to your liking
5. Save your changes

Explanation of Each Preference and Setting

1. **Image Resolution:** This setting allows you to set the resolution of the image generated.

2. **Stylize Values:** Here you can adjust the stylize values to get the desired look and feel of the image.

3. **Quality Commands:** This setting allows you to adjust the quality of the image.

4. **URL Inspiration:** With this setting, you can use URLs as inspiration for your images.

5. **Text Weights:** You can use this setting to adjust the weight of text in your images.

6. **Output File Format:** This setting allows you to choose the format in which the image will be saved.

Examples of Each Preference and Setting in Use

1. **Image Resolution:** If you want your image to be in high resolution, you can set the image resolution to "High".

2. **Stylize Values**: If you want a more realistic look and feel, you can adjust the stylize values to "Natural".

3. **Quality Commands:** If you want your image to have the highest quality, you can set the quality commands to "High".

4. URL Inspiration: If you have an image that you want to use as inspiration for your own, you can enter the URL in the URL Inspiration setting.

5. Text Weights: If you want your text to be bold and stand out, you can set the text weights to "Bold".

6. Output File Format: If you want your image to be saved as a .png file, you can set the output file format to ".png".

9

A Brief History of Midjourney AI

Midjourney AI is a relatively new platform in the world of artificial intelligence and machine learning. The company behind the platform was founded in 2019 by a team of computer scientists, data engineers, and machine learning experts who saw the potential of AI to transform the way we create and interact with digital media.

The idea for Midjourney AI came from the team's experience with other AI-powered platforms, which they felt were too complex and difficult for beginners to use. They wanted to create a platform that would be accessible and easy to use, even for people with no experience in machine learning or programming.

The team started working on Midjourney AI in early 2019, and by the end of the year, they had launched the first version of the platform. The initial version focused on image generation, using deep learning models to create realistic and high-quality images from simple prompts.

The response to the platform was overwhelmingly positive, with users praising the ease of use and the quality of the generated images. The team continued to refine and improve the platform over the following months, adding new features and capabilities to make it even more powerful and flexible.

In 2020, the team launched a major update to the platform, adding support for video creation and expanding the range of image generation styles and techniques. They also introduced a new pricing model that made the platform more accessible and affordable for individuals and small businesses.

Today, Midjourney AI is one of the most popular and widely used AI-powered media creation platforms, with thousands of users around the world. The platform continues to evolve and improve, with new features and capabilities being added on a regular basis.

Despite its relative youth, Midjourney AI has already had a significant impact on the world of digital media, enabling creators of all levels of experience to produce high-quality, visually stunning content with ease. As AI and machine learning continue to advance, it's likely that Midjourney AI will play an increasingly important role in the future of media creation and consumption.

10

Examples

One of the best ways to learn how to use Midjourney AI is to see examples of it in action. In this chapter, we'll look at some examples of how to use Midjourney AI to create different types of content.

Creating an Abstract Art Piece

In this example, we'll show you how to use Midjourney AI to create a unique and eye-catching abstract art piece. Abstract art is a popular genre that relies on color, shape, and form to create non-representational images that evoke emotions and ideas. Midjourney AI can be a powerful tool for creating abstract art, allowing you to experiment with different styles, color palettes, and shapes.

To start, we'll need to input our prompts. For this example, we'll use a single prompt: **"colorful abstract art."** We'll also select the multi-prompt option, which will allow Midjourney AI to generate a wider range of visual possibilities.

Next, we'll adjust the parameters. We'll set the stylize value to "abstract," which will help create a more stylized and non-representational image. We'll also adjust the quality settings to generate a high-resolution image that captures the details of the abstract forms and colors.

Once the prompts and parameters are set, we can generate the image. Midjourney AI will analyze the input data and generate a unique abstract art piece that incorporates the colors and shapes of the input prompt. The image will likely have a range of different shapes, colors, and textures, creating a vibrant and dynamic visual experience.

To further refine the image, we can adjust the parameters and quality settings. We might experiment with different stylize values, such as "painted" or "pop art," to create a different visual style. We can also adjust the quality settings to generate a larger or smaller image, depending on our needs.

Overall, using Midjourney AI to create abstract art is a fun and rewarding process. By experimenting with different prompts and parameters, we can create unique and visually striking images that reflect our creative vision. With the right prompts and parameters, the possibilities are endless!

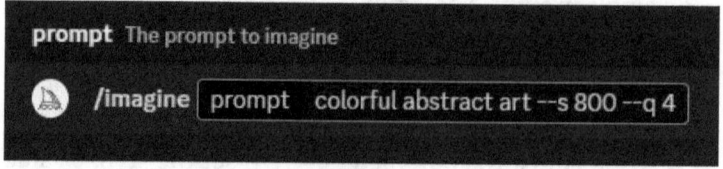

* * *

Generating a Realistic Landscape

In this example, we'll show you how to use Midjourney AI to create a stunningly realistic landscape. Realistic landscapes are a popular genre in visual art, and Midjourney AI can be a powerful tool for generating images that capture the beauty and complexity of nature.

To start, we'll need to input our prompts. For this example, we'll use a combination of text prompts and URLs. Our text prompt will be "**realistic landscape**," and we'll also input URLs

59

for photos of real-world landscapes that we find inspiring. {In this example I used: https://upload.wikimedia.org/wikipedia/commons/9/91/Maldonado_desde_la_Barra.jpg}

Next, we'll adjust the parameters. We'll set the stylize value to "realistic," which will help create an image that captures the nuances of light and shadow, as well as the textures and colors of natural landscapes. We'll also adjust the quality settings to generate a high-resolution image that captures the details of the landscape.

Once the prompts and parameters are set, we can generate the image. Midjourney AI will analyze the input data and generate a unique landscape image that incorporates the features of the input prompts and URLs. The image will likely have a range of natural elements, such as mountains, trees, and water, that create a sense of depth and realism.

To further refine the image, we can adjust the parameters and quality settings. We might experiment with different stylize values, such as "painterly" or "watercolor," to create a different visual style. We can also adjust the quality settings to generate a larger or smaller image, depending on our needs.

Using URLs for inspiration can be particularly useful for generating realistic landscapes, as it allows us to draw on a broad range of visual content from the web. By experimenting with different URLs and adjusting the parameters, we can create unique and visually stunning landscape images that capture the beauty and complexity of the natural world.

Overall, using Midjourney AI to generate realistic landscapes is a powerful tool for creating visually stunning images. By experimenting with different prompts and parameters, we can create images that reflect our creative vision and capture the beauty and complexity of the natural world.

By following these examples and playing around with the prompts and parameters, you'll gain a better understanding of how to use Midjourney AI to create the content you want.

11

Practice

In order to truly master Midjourney AI, it's important to practice using the platform regularly. In this chapter, we'll go through some practice exercises that you can do to improve your skills.

Prompt Creation

One of the most important parts of using Midjourney AI is creating effective prompts. Prompts are the input data that guide the image or video generation process, and a well-crafted prompt can make all the difference in the quality and style of the output.

To create effective prompts, start by choosing a subject or theme that you want to explore. This could be anything from a specific object, like a tree or a building, to a broader concept, like "nostalgia" or "adventure." Once you have a subject or theme in mind, brainstorm a list of related words, phrases, or images that could be used as prompts.

Experiment with different prompt structures and combinations to see what works best for your specific needs. For example, you might use a single text prompt, a combination of text and image prompts, or even a set of prompts that change over time to create a dynamic image or video.

Here are a few examples of prompt structures and combinations that can be used in Midjourney AI:

Text Prompts

These are simple, one-word or short phrase prompts that describe the subject or theme you want to explore. For example, if you want to generate an image of a forest, your text prompts might include "trees," "woods," "nature," and "green."

Image Prompts

These are URLs or uploaded images that you use as visual inspiration for the image or video generation process. For example, if you want to generate an image of a beach, you might input URLs for photos of beaches that you find inspiring.

Multi-Prompts

This is a feature in Midjourney AI that allows you to input multiple prompts at once, creating a more complex and nuanced image or video. For example, if you want to generate an image of a mountain range, you might input a combination of text prompts, such as "mountains," "scenic," and "landscape," as well as image prompts for photos of mountain ranges.

Experimenting with different prompt structures and combinations can help you create unique and visually stunning images or videos in Midjourney AI. By carefully crafting your prompts, you can guide the image or video generation process and achieve the desired style and tone for your creative vision.

Parameter Adjustment

Parameter adjustment is an essential part of the Midjourney AI image or video generation process. Parameters control various aspects of the output, such as the style, color, and quality of the image or video. Adjusting the parameters can help you achieve the desired look and feel for your creative vision.

To adjust the parameters in Midjourney AI, start by generating an image or video using your chosen prompts. Once you have an output that you like, try experimenting with different parameter settings to see how they affect the output. Here are a few examples of parameter adjustments that you can make in Midjourney AI:

Style
The stylize value in Midjourney AI controls the degree of stylization in the output. A lower value produces more realistic images or videos, while a higher value produces more stylized or abstract results. Experiment with different stylize values to achieve the desired level of stylization.

Color
The color command in Midjourney AI allows you to adjust the color scheme of the output. You can use the color command to change the color of specific elements in the image or video, or to

create an entirely new color scheme. Experiment with different color values and settings to achieve the desired color scheme.

Quality

The quality command in Midjourney AI controls the resolution and compression of the output. A higher quality setting produces a larger and more detailed image or video, while a lower quality setting produces a smaller and less detailed output. Experiment with different quality settings to achieve the desired resolution and level of detail.

Other Parameters

Midjourney AI includes a range of other parameters that can be adjusted to fine-tune the output. For example, the crop command can be used to adjust the cropping and composition of the output, while the noise command can be used to add texture and detail to the image or video.

By experimenting with different parameter settings, you can achieve a range of different styles, tones, and visual effects in your Midjourney AI outputs. Take an existing output and try adjusting the parameters to see how it affects the final product. With practice and experimentation, you can fine-tune your outputs to achieve the desired results for your creative vision.

Style Exploration

One of the most exciting parts of using Midjourney AI is exploring the various styles available for image and video generation. Each style has a unique look and feel, ranging from realistic to abstract, and exploring different styles can help you achieve the desired tone and visual effect for your creative vision.

To explore different styles in Midjourney AI, start by choosing a style that you haven't used before. For example, you might try the "impressionist" style for a painting-like effect, or the "sketch" style for a hand-drawn look. Once you have chosen a style, input your prompts and generate an image or video using that style.

After generating the output, take a moment to compare it to other styles you've used before. What are the differences in the look and feel of the output? How does the new style affect the overall tone and visual effect of the output? Experiment with different styles to see how they can be used to create different types of content.

Here are a few examples of how different styles can be used in Midjourney AI:

Realistic

Realistic styles, such as "default" and "natural," are great for generating images or videos that accurately represent reality. These styles can be used for product photography, landscapes, or other types of content that require a high level of accuracy and detail.

66

Abstract

Abstract styles, such as "drip" or "impressionist," can be used to create visually striking images or videos that have a more artistic or surreal feel. These styles are great for creating artwork, or for adding a unique visual element to a project.

Cartoon

Cartoon styles, such as "cartoon" or "pencil," can be used to create animated or playful images or videos. These styles are great for creating characters, logos, or other types of content that require a fun and lighthearted tone.

By exploring different styles in Midjourney AI, you can expand your creative horizons and discover new ways to achieve the desired tone and visual effect for your projects. Try different styles and see how they can be used to create a range of visually stunning and engaging content.

By practicing these exercises and exploring the platform, you'll gain a deeper understanding of how Midjourney AI works and how to use it to create the content you want.

12

Bonus: Tips and Tricks

If you're looking to get the most out of Midjourney AI, there are a few tips and tricks that can help you achieve better results. In this chapter, we'll go over some of the best tips and tricks for using the platform.

Use URLs for Inspiration

URLs can be a great source of inspiration for generating images or videos. Try using URLs for images or videos that you like to inspire your own creations.URLs can be a rich source of inspiration for generating new images and videos, as they allow you to draw on a vast pool of digital content from across the web.

Using URLs in Midjourney AI is a simple process. When setting up a new project, you can input one or more URLs for images or videos that you like, or that you want your generated content to resemble. Midjourney AI will then use these URLs to analyze the content and generate new images or videos that incorporate similar features or themes.

For example, let's say you're creating a project to generate images of landscapes. You can input URLs for photos of real-world landscapes that you find inspiring, such as those from nature blogs or travel websites. Midjourney AI will then use these URLs to generate new landscape images that incorporate similar features, such as color palettes, composition, and texture.

The ability to use URLs for inspiration can be particularly useful for artists, designers, and marketers who need to create visual content that aligns with specific brand or project requirements. By drawing on a broad range of visual content from the web, they can generate new images or videos that capture the essence of their brand or project, while still being original and creative.

Overall, using URLs for inspiration is a powerful tool for unlocking new creative possibilities in Midjourney AI. By exploring and experimenting with different URLs, you can discover new ideas and inspiration that you might not have found otherwise, and use them to create stunning, original content.

Adjust Parameters for Quality

To achieve the best results, it's important to understand how to adjust the parameters in Midjourney AI to optimize the quality of the output.

There are several parameters in Midjourney AI that can be

adjusted to control the quality of the output, such as resolution, aspect ratio, and compression. By experimenting with different settings for these parameters, you can achieve the desired level of quality for your specific needs.

For example, let's say you're creating a project to generate images for a high-end print publication. In this case, you would want to ensure that the images are generated at a high resolution, with sharp details and vibrant colors. To achieve this, you would need to adjust the resolution and color parameters in Midjourney AI to optimize for high-quality output.

On the other hand, if you're creating a project to generate images for a web page or social media post, you might prioritize faster processing and smaller file sizes over ultra-high resolution. In this case, you would need to adjust the compression and aspect ratio parameters to optimize for fast processing and smaller file sizes.

The key to adjusting parameters for quality in Midjourney AI is to experiment with different settings and evaluate the results until you find the best balance between quality and processing speed for your specific needs. By taking the time to fine-tune the parameters, you can achieve the best possible results for your projects.

Overall, adjusting parameters for quality is a powerful tool for achieving the desired results in Midjourney AI. By understanding how to adjust the parameters for your specific needs, you can create stunning, high-quality images and videos that meet your creative and professional goals.

Save and Reuse Prompts

The quality of the output can be greatly enhanced by using effective prompts. Prompts are input data that are used by Midjourney AI to generate new images and videos. Examples of prompts include keywords, text descriptions, and URLs.

If you find a set of prompts that work well for you, you can save them for later use. This can save you time and help you generate consistent results. Midjourney AI provides the ability to save and organize your prompts, making it easy to reuse them in future projects.

For example, let's say you're a photographer who frequently uses Midjourney AI to generate images for your website or portfolio. You might have a set of prompts that you use to generate a specific style of image that is consistent with your brand or artistic style. By saving these prompts in a folder, you can easily access them for future projects, saving time and ensuring consistency in your visual content.

Similarly, if you work in marketing or design, you might have a set of prompts that you use to generate images or videos for specific products or campaigns. By saving these prompts in a folder, you can easily reuse them for future campaigns, ensuring consistency in your brand messaging and visual style.

The ability to save and reuse prompts is a powerful tool for creating consistent, high-quality content in Midjourney AI. By organizing and reusing effective prompts, you can save time, increase efficiency, and ensure that your visual content aligns with your brand or artistic style.

Overall, saving and reusing prompts is a key strategy for achieving success in Midjourney AI. By taking the time to develop and organize effective prompts, you can create stunning, high-quality images and videos that meet your creative and professional goals.

By following these tips and tricks, you can take your Midjourney AI creations to the next level.

13

Conclusion

Recap of Midjourney AI

In this book, we have explored the exciting world of Midjourney AI, a powerful tool for creating stunning images. We have covered the basics of the software, including the frequently used commands, the different types of parameters and stylize values, and the various quality commands. We also learned how to use URLs for inspiration and how to adjust text weights, as well as how to access and use preferences and settings.

Final thoughts on using Midjourney AI

With its ease of use and versatility, Midjourney AI is an excellent tool for creating beautiful images. Whether you're a professional designer or just someone who loves to create art, Midjourney AI is an excellent choice for unleashing your creativity. With the knowledge and skills you've gained from this book, you should be well on your way to creating amazing images that will amaze and inspire others.

Additional resources for learning Midjourney AI

While this book has provided a comprehensive introduction to Midjourney AI, there's always more to learn. The best way to become a pro at using the software is to dive in and start experimenting! However, there are also numerous online resources and tutorials that can help you expand your skills and knowledge. Be sure to explore the software's official website and forums, as well as YouTube and other video sharing platforms, for more tips and tricks on using Midjourney AI.

14

Glossary

Artificial Intelligence (AI): A branch of computer science that focuses on creating intelligent machines that can perform tasks that typically require human intelligence, such as visual perception, speech recognition, and decision-making.

Deep Learning: A subset of machine learning that uses neural networks to analyze large amounts of data and identify patterns that can be used to make predictions or generate new content.

Image Generation: The process of using AI or machine learning algorithms to generate new images from prompts or other input data.

Machine Learning: A branch of AI that focuses on creating algorithms that can learn from and make predictions based on data, without being explicitly programmed to do so.

Midjourney AI: An AI-powered platform for media creation that uses deep learning algorithms to generate images and videos from prompts and other input data.

Multi-Prompts: A feature in Midjourney AI that allows users to input multiple prompts at once, allowing for more complex and nuanced image or video generation.

Negative Prompt Weights: Parameters in Midjourney AI that allow users to specify certain prompts to be ignored when generating images or videos. This can be useful for removing unwanted elements or creating specific visual effects.

Parameters: Settings that can be adjusted in Midjourney AI to control various aspects of the image or video generation process, such as style, color, and quality.

Prompts: Input data that is used by Midjourney AI to generate images or videos. Prompts can take many forms, such as text, keywords, or images.

Quality: A parameter in Midjourney AI that controls the level of detail and fidelity in the generated images or videos.

Style Transfer: A technique in image generation that involves taking the style of one image and applying it to another image. Midjourney AI uses style transfer algorithms to create unique and visually stunning images.

Stylize Values: Parameters in Midjourney AI that control the style of the generated images or videos, such as the level of abstraction or the degree of realism.

Text Weights: A parameter in Midjourney AI that allows users to adjust the importance of different text prompts in the image or video generation process. This can be useful for creating images or videos with a specific tone or message.

Training Data: The data used to train the machine learning algorithms in Midjourney AI. This data can include a wide range of visual content, such as photos, videos, and other images.

Transfer Learning: A technique in machine learning that involves reusing pre-trained models or datasets to solve new problems. Midjourney AI uses transfer learning to create more efficient and effective algorithms for image and video generation.

URLs: Uniform Resource Locators, or web addresses, that can be used in Midjourney AI as prompts to generate images or videos based on content found on the internet.

User Interface (UI): The visual interface that users interact with when using Midjourney AI. The UI allows users to input prompts, adjust parameters, and generate images and videos. A well-designed UI can greatly improve the user experience and make it easier to achieve the desired results.

Video Generation: The process of using AI or machine learning algorithms to generate new videos from prompts or other input data.

Hopefully, this glossary will help you better understand the key terms and concepts related to Midjourney AI.

About the Author

Avery Wright is an enigmatic figure who is an author in the fields of AI, Technology, and the Arts. A combat veteran of the US Army, Avery has almost two decades of experience in the IT industry, which has given them a unique perspective on the intersection of technology and society.

As an author, Avery has published a range of books on topics such as the future of AI, the role of drones in modern warfare, and the medicinal properties of mushrooms. Their writing often explores the cutting-edge of technology and how it is changing the world around us. Avery's work is notable for its depth and insight, as well as its ability to make complex topics accessible to a broad audience.

Away from the world of writing, Avery is a private individual who values their privacy. Despite this, they remain a voice in the tech industry and beyond. Whether sharing their thoughts on the latest developments in AI or commenting on the state of the world, Avery's perspective is always worth listening to.

You can connect with me on:

🌐 https://sirexodia.wixsite.com/avery-wright

🐦 https://twitter.com/AveryWrightAI

📘 https://www.facebook.com/profile.php?id=100089987171726

🔗 https://www.amazon.com/author/averywrightai

Subscribe to my newsletter:

✉ https://sirexodia.wixsite.com/avery-wright

Also by Avery Wright

Avery Wright's work spans a range of topics, from the cutting-edge of AI and technology to the ancient practice of Taoism and the art of chess. Their books are notable for their depth, insight, and ability to make complex topics accessible to a broad audience. With almost two decades of experience in the IT field and a background as a combat veteran, Avery brings a unique perspective to their writing that is both informative and thought-provoking. Whether you are interested in exploring the frontiers of technology or deepening your understanding of the human experience, Avery's books are a must-read.

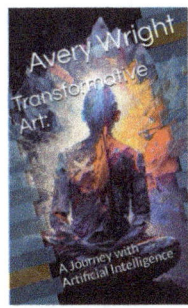

Transformative Art - A Journey with Artificial Intelligence
Transformative Art: A Journey with AI is a visually stunning and thought-provoking book that explores the intersection of artificial intelligence and the world of art. The book features breathtaking images of futuristic cities, technology, vehicles, robots, flying ships, conceptual art, abstract art, and unique pieces, all within the context of transformative art. Each chapter begins with a powerful quote that sets the tone for a deep dive into the themes of perception, change, reflection, risk-taking, emotional connection, the journey within, and the universal language of art. The book is written by Avery Wright, a talented author with a passion for exploring the ways in which technology is changing our lives and our world. This book is a must-read for anyone interested in the intersection of art, technology, and the human experience. https://www.amazon.com/dp/B0BTWNYLJD

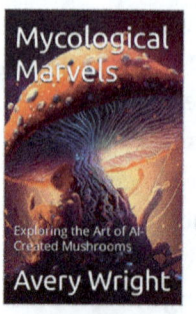

Mycological Marvels: Exploring the Art of AI-Created Mushrooms

Mycological Marvels: Exploring the Art of AI-Created Mushrooms" showcases stunning AI-generated mushroom art and delves into the technical & creative aspects of this innovative form of art. A celebration of beauty & technology in the world of art.

https://www.amazon.com/dp/B0BVFS2MNX

Chat GPT: A Digital Journey Begins

ChatGPT: A Digital Journey Begins" is the first book in an exciting series that takes readers on a journey into the world of artificial intelligence and natural language processing. Through the development and evolution of ChatGPT, readers will gain an in-depth understanding of the complex and sophisticated technology that powers this groundbreaking model. From the creation of the neural network to the potential applications of ChatGPT in various fields, this book provides a comprehensive and fascinating overview of one of the most innovative and exciting technological advancements of our time.

https://www.amazon.com/dp/B0BVQB5M91

Unleashing ChatGPT's Power: Navigating the Digital Realm

"Unleashing ChatGPT's Power: Navigating the Digital Realm" explores the complex and sophisticated technology behind one of the most innovative and exciting technological advancements of our time. Through in-depth discussions of the underlying technology that powers ChatGPT, its ability to process natural language, and its expanding knowledge base, readers will gain a deeper understanding of the ways in which artificial intelligence and natural language processing are shaping the future of society.

https://www.amazon.com/dp/B0BVSYQ77H

The Tao of Inner Peace

The Tao of Inner Peace is an introduction to the ancient Chinese philosophy and religion of Taoism. This book explores the core teachings of Taoism and how they can be applied in everyday life to find inner peace and harmony. The book covers a range of topics, including the concept of Tao, the Yin-Yang philosophy, the Tao Te Ching, living in harmony with nature, the Tao of relationships, and the Tao in action. With practical guidance and advice, this book will help readers cultivate a more peaceful and fulfilling life by adopting a Taoist approach to everyday living."

https://www.amazon.com/dp/B0BVMJ83DZ

Taoism Unleashed: Advanced Concepts for Deepening Your Practice

"Taoism Unleashed: Advanced Concepts for Deepening Your Practice" is a comprehensive guide to advanced Taoist concepts, designed to help readers deepen their practice and cultivate greater levels of inner peace, balance, and harmony. Through exploring the concepts of energy flow, chakras, meditation, exercise techniques, and advanced Taoist philosophy, this book offers practical tools and techniques for achieving greater levels of physical health, emotional well-being, and spiritual growth. With a focus on practical, everyday applications, "Taoism Unleashed" provides readers with the tools and insights they need to unleash their true potential and achieve a deeper connection to the Tao.

https://www.amazon.com/dp/B0BVL8G42H

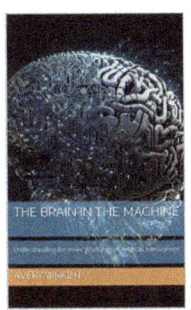

The Brain in the Machine: Understanding the Inner Workings of Artificial Intelligence (Mastering AI)

"The Brain in the Machine: Understanding the Inner Workings of Artificial Intelligence" provides a comprehensive and accessible introduction to the field of artificial intelligence. From the history of AI to the latest advances in deep learning, natural language processing, and computer vision, this book covers a wide range of topics to help readers understand the inner workings of AI. With a focus on the practical applications of AI, this book is an ideal resource for students, researchers, and practitioners in the field.

https://www.amazon.com/dp/B0BW6FGRTK